A SUITE OF ANGELS

and other poems

A SUITE OF ANGELS

and other poems

by

Kenneth Pitchford

The University of North Carolina Press
Chapel Hill

Copyright © 1957, 1959, 1961, 1962, 1963, 1964, 1965, 1966, 1967
by Kenneth Pitchford

CONTEMPORARY POETRY SERIES

Some of the poems in this book have previously appeared in *Best Poems of 1963, Carolina Quarterly, The Carleton Miscellany, Chelsea Review, Chicago Review, Envoi, The Kenyon Review, The Massachusetts Review, The New Republic, The NYU Supplement, Poems by Seven, Outposts, Poetry Northwest, The Saturday Review, Shenandoah, The Transatlantic Review, The Various Light*, and *Quarterly Review of Literature*. Section 6 of "A Suite of Angels" originally appeared as "The Queen" in *The New Yorker*. "Ariadne with Child" originally appeared as "Heraklion" in *Poetry*. "Farewell in a Dry Summer" was set to music by Lockrem Johnson and published by Dow Music Publishers. "Song for Lying in Bed During a Night Rain" was set to music by Ned Rorem as a portion of his song cycle, *Poems of Love and the Rain*, published by Boosey and Hawkes and recorded on Composers Recordings, Inc.

Library of Congress Catalog Card Number 67-17029
Printed by The North Carolina State Print Shop, Raleigh
Manufactured in the United States of America

for ALLEN TATE

CONTENTS

I

A SUITE OF ANGELS 3
THE CHILDREN 11
TWO LIVES 13
DURING CONSTRUCTION 15
ARIADNE WITH CHILD 16
CONJURY 17

II

AN ARRAIGNMENT 23
THE CANDIDATE'S DREAM 25
IS AND IS NOT 26
THE COURTIER 27
EMISSARY FROM A WAR 29
A BIRTH 30

III

THREE VISITATIONS 33
TRAGIC ARCH 35
EAGLE AND SPARROW 37
THE WER-MAN 38

THE TOUR 40
HOMECOMINGS 41

IV

THE DECORATORS 47
FAREWELL IN A DRY SUMMER 49
FUN HOUSE 50
UNDER NEW MANAGEMENT 51
SERAPHIC COMBAT 52
MEETING 53

V

DOWNHILL 57
ROUGHING IT 59
SONG FOR LYING IN BED DURING
A NIGHT RAIN 61
RITES OF PASSAGE 62
MOVING OUT 63
THE BULL-KILLER 65

VI

NIGHTMARES 71

I

And where Love's form is, Love is; Love is form.
—Chapman

A SUITE OF ANGELS

1—The God

I am sunlight before your leaded glass
shatters me into color. Stiff saints praying
within their stony wilderness encase
only a tinted becoming. I am being.

And as the mirror held to catch the sun
reflects but a blurred surprise, your clearest silver
taints with shadow what in me no stain
can mar. You sense me as a chill—and shiver.

Heavy with me, your silences create
music and magic, dreams that weave toward myth.
Barren, I hang gold fruit on your branching sight.
My spawn swim upstream bleeding. I am death.

2—The Minister

"Look where you've stopped the car," she laughed and pointed
to the church across from them. The bleary lieutenant
belched and leaned across the seat. "They never lock
the doors. The minister who confirmed me died
not long after. But that was years ago."

She had been first to point out his resemblance
to the Gabriel in the stained-glass annunciation
on the pulpit's left. Everyone agreed
the profiles matched but when the new minister's
full face leaned above them, resemblance vanished.

His brows grew together as no angel's should,
the backs of his hands were blurred by clouds of hair,
and a wisp or two curled upward to surmount
even the crisp white circle about his neck.
Her father himself had hardly so dense a beard.

She recalled too well her troubled audience.
"It's not just my father don't believe,"—her tears
obscuring how the hair on his hands and brow

grew beaded as they talked in the drafty chancel—
"but that my angels don't come back no more."

Lieutenant, minister, both seemed the same to her now,
the once on a darkening Friday in black vestment,
here at two a.m. by moonlight. "Why not
go in a minute with me? I want to see
if it's still the same." The lieutenant laughed and followed.

Inside, the dark shapes in the glass grew clear
after a minute's peering. Dazed faces stared
above her in profile as they had in childhood.
"They had so much more color then," she said,
as the soldier's moist hands searched and tugged until

she lay on the chancel carpet where she saw,
turned upside down, her gray annunciation.

> 3—The Sister
>
> Being brotherless, I grew to love
>   the sister I had feared.
> She, being older, could complicate
>   every game we played.
>
> Though I was her spy, she was God's.
>   Ghosts and angels appeared
> whenever she chose to call. Their talk
>   became our daily bread.
>
> My earliest task was to interrupt
>   the love our parents made,
> not knowing how fiercely she wanted
>   what the wife in that dark room had.
>
> The angels that surrounded us
>   in *our* bed did not guard
> their nightly offices. Demons writhed
>   to watch the games they played.
>
> But when she, too, had learned first hand
>   the trick she'd been denied,

angels no longer visited,
    pale ghosts grew afraid.

  How desperately she must have opened
    to soldiers who have died
  her body's treasures, pretending passion
    the one rule she obeyed.

  The ranking lover courted me,
    as well, in the calls he paid,
  as though he might have guessed what the fee
    usurped and whom it gulled.

  So she procured me brothers and slept
    no more as once she had,
  with him who'd eavesdropped on her first love
    while all her angels sighed.

4—The King

The day had threatened thunder. Having washed
the marks of the slaughterhouse from my face and hands,
I rolled down my spattered sleeves and walked
out to the highway, hoping to catch a ride

into the city before the spring rains could break.
Reading Bulfinch and thumbing what few cars passed,
I quaked as each new sheet of lightning scoured
the tarnished clouds. Then the late rasp of thunder.

"What are you reading?" an old man asked, surprising
my gaze, throwing open the door to the rickety car
that pulled up, unbeckoned, beside the gray stretch of road.
"About Zeus," I told him, "who came as a swan,

or an eagle, or a bull, or a golden shower." "Get in,"
he said. "I'll drive you into town before
the rain." And we said nothing more while the car
coughed along the asphalt, until the man

looked over at his passenger miles later.
"Zeus. That's interesting. Bit of a reader

myself. What've *you* been doing out here?"
"I've been killing animals all day,"

I explained. "Uh huh," the man mused. "Zeus. That's strange.
The fact is, He can wear any kind of body whatso-
ever, as we might casually wear an amulet
around the throat, free to put it on

and take it off as often as He wishes."
While he talked, the rains fell—in slashes across
the windshield, nothing clear beyond the peeling
ration stamp and a St. Christopher

that swayed against the blinded glass. "Today,"
I said in my thin boy's voice, "we killed
a big bull who wouldn't be still, but reared and spurted
blood at us until we'd shot him half-a-dozen times."

"When the lightnings glare and are gone that announce His coming,"
the driver continued, "I try to be content.
You see, the God once wore my body too,
though only once, a split second, and never after."

At least we don't kill birds there, I thought, not guessing
why I shrank from listening to his talk,
alarmed to recall, instead, the time my father
had brought three mallards home from a day's hunt,

and how I'd trembled to watch my sister clean them,
spattering the white enamel table,
while we heard the muffled sounds of struggle
that came in creaks and whispers from the next room.

"My son," the driver began, the city's outskirts
rising up gray about us— "Thanks, this is fine,"
I answered, leaping out the door to hurtle
across the pavement and dash home through the rain.

That night, still feverish from my drenching, I dreamt
I walked obscured within a halo of birds
across morasses of dying animals
to the porch of an empty house where I stood naked

but for a medallion pulsing at my throat.
Then I heard a scuffling within and saw
a great bull come charging through the open doorway,
horned bright as lightning, blood coursing from his withers.

And saw beyond, before the bull could wake me,
my father asleep with the old man in his arms.

5—The Husband

He wrestled till the carefree dead
surrendered their secrets, yet no stone
yielded a hollow for his bared
skull once the shocks of battle ran

his body through no more. He bled
inwardly, without a sign
to tell how like a crimson braid
his scar would live and glow unseen.

When he returned, he took to bed
the woman who had loved the slain,
and he alone escaped to build
sons from a daughter of mere men.

But always in the love they made,
he knew how her light-blazoned skin
became the field he learned to dread,
the place of death his wrestling won.

Across his flesh her lips deployed
their red insignia, to gain
back all her murdered. Thus arrayed,
he wept, but slaughtered them again.

6—The Queen

Always before, we sped in the same direction,
not even aware we moved until the opposing train
swayed alongside. Then we saw
how full of arcs and spirals our course
webbed out before us: one train dipping

as the second rose out of sight to reappear
on the other side, so that we sat a foot apart
peering into each other's lives.

Sometimes when I regained the upper air
I might look about expecting to see you
ascending the stair a second later,
but we met only underground,
both our trains hissing as though to strike
our illusory single destination
just ahead in the darkness,
like the intertwining bodies of two snakes.

We met thus often; you never read
a paper or book or even the printed furrow
of my time's madness above us,
always wearing the same unpleated blue,
wheat-colored hair drawn back by a single comb.
Whenever I saw you, you were already looking
into my gaze as long as the trains allowed.
Perhaps we invented each other. Neither smiled.

Here, this first winter day, I see you motionless
on the opposite platform, waiting as I,
but now for a train that runs the other way.
Again, you have already seen me when I notice,
but neither goes to the stairway that would lead
to the other's landing. We only stand and cast
a spiderweb of intersecting gazes,
less beautiful than those our courses wove.

I spin your history: sister, Persephone,
still wearing the color of her fields and skies,
making her stately progress across the river
into the kingdom of sleepless sleep. And yet
I wonder why you rode so long beside me
to break away forever now, at the season's turning.
I could not be your king except where dreams erupt
through an uprooted aconite in a field

real trains never reach. As a hiss of brakes
heralds your car's arrival
and our brittle net shatters in sympathy,

we wave goodbye, our only recognition,
until our trains curve back upon each other a last time,
you on the way to our impossible meadow
where the springtime's bridegroom waits,
I on my last descent into the dark.

7—The Angel

After so long an absence, why
should the angel visit me,
instead of that woman out of whose
profoundest need he first arose?

So I wondered. Yet there he stood,
his polished body honed and bared,
its molten silver like a shield
enclosing the gold flesh I beheld.

Annunciation's ritual
prevented speech. From neither fell
a recognition that he had seen
the presence he intruded on.

Our gazes locked as in the game
children play when they assume
stone postures to outwatch a friend.
But we were easy in that bond.

I heard behind him in the dark
bulls snuffling; above, the quick
cries of wounded birds; beneath,
snakes hissing within the earth.

In back of me, I heard the sigh
of lovers fading as they lay
touching the scar none can erase,
the line of distance between their kiss.

"Angel," I said at last, "to look
through the skin's film is but to break
into a darkened room in hell
where beast and man alike are foul.

You have shown me every love
I thought I chose was but a hive
within which father and sister slept.
In thirty years I've not escaped."

The angel, sad that I should speak,
turned from me and with a shake
of his great pinions disappeared.
Beast voices, mourning him, grew loud.

But he stands yet, somewhere between
a woman I will not know again
and all my fear: his single shape
guards us in our double sleep.

THE CHILDREN

With thin shifts knotted about their waists,
   the two children splashed in the water,
while beyond the vineyard where chattering jays
   pecked at the yellow grapes, their fathers
conferred about the building of the maze.

They wrestled as equals, the boy without beard,
   the girl brief-breasted and downy,
then lay at last on the grass and shared
   an hour's embrace, still and sunny,
though the whole time neither said a word.

Half-drowsing, she thought how her fallen fist
   across his hip might startle
the bird that nested there, she guessed,
   and send it flying for the gold portal
in the blue tunnel of the sky it crossed.

He, half-waking, wondered what hush
   the other mouth had not yet broken
that lay sealed from his tensing flesh,
   or if a fringed eye might awaken
between those lids and stare to stone his wish

   for paths admitting him. But she
     laughed suddenly, and rising,
   they walked along the bank to see
     the calf her brother, where he lay dozing,
then woke him up, climbed on, and rode away.

He carried them into the half-domed maze,
   though the walls were taller
than they themselves could see across,
   even from their perch. His collar
tinkled as they moved into fuller darkness.

"I'm getting off," the girl fearfully cried
   and clambered down. But the other,
stirred by the feel of matted hide

between his thighs, nipped them tighter
and nudged the calf into a quicker stride.

"I'm lost, don't leave me." But they galloped past.
   She looked about in shadow.
"Father should jail them all," she mused,
as the hoofbeats dwindled beneath a chatter
of jays in the vineyard, reminding her of her thirst.

She walked an hour, then stumbled over
   what turned her eyes to stone,
and made her wish for a beast-legged lover
   with blazing wings whose sword might rend
the loathsome thing she saw forever:

the boy and sleeping beast entwined,
   the boy's mouth closed on the grizzled
member of the calf who grinned,
   hooves spread, while in the vineyard, sun-dazzled,
the hulls of fallen grapes despoiled the ground.

TWO LIVES

She strove to rehearse his habits like a play
and miss each cue with practiced negligence;
the days were long, yet his evenings with the paper
crept gracelessly across her cooling gaze.
She wanted no fresh flowers in the house,
or to burn a pie, or leave the bed unmade—

> He was content to read the evening paper
> and settle himself into a daily round
> answering to nothing but the season's
> raising of misty airs or snows or rains
> for his alarmclock rising or evening whistle
> that brought him safely through the dangerous years.

—but always some face or fact, some passing stranger,
some urchin chalking Poison on the sidewalk
would soften every will she sought to harden
until she set right more things than were wrong
and simply shrugged to see her abstract longings
spell out, like living runes, their single word.

> For one night in the bedroom as he leaned
> to kick his shoes off and turn back the sheet,
> he saw a motto on their pressed-board wall,
> one she had hung that morning: God is Love.

His kitchen meals beside the radio
were tuned to overhearing the usual frenzies:
someone deported, shot, official protest,
demand, refusal, reply. He scarcely heard.
All slipped away behind some other thought
that lay like shadow landscapes in his mind—

> The windowledge with three tomatoes precisely
> laid to ripen became her nemesis,
> a blond unhurried giving and forgiving,
> but when his nights demanded her in flesh
> only the moon's long look through their bedroom curtains
> brought near the greater distance of her kiss.

—something beyond the sky's soot-blackened branches
he saw from the windows of his factory,
something beyond the times that she forgot
to bring the paper in or would not speak.
He heard a constant chant that never claimed him
in any language he had ever used.

  One washday, draining the last laundry tub,
  she found his favorite pipe and scooping it up,
  a driftwood stick of habit, a broken life,
  she wept among the half-hung steaming clothes.

DURING CONSTRUCTION

As the barely afforded house was being built,
   we went at sundown to find it lying
      in thawed lakes of clay,
   like a hulk beached there, dead or dying,
its skeleton seen through the ruptures of a pelt
      only partly eaten away.

Of course it was death's opposite we saw:
   our father who'd helped to build it clambered
      before us up the stair.
   It had been morning since he'd hammered
the slanting beams where undereaves would grow
      the rooms we were to share.

"This will be yours, Norma, here, and this is Ken's."
   We walked gingerly past each rafter,
      through a smell of pine just cut.
   In the middle of her room, though, our laughter
froze when we saw, hung from those wooden bones,
      the dark sack of a bat—

as though it were the ribbed heart of the house,
   charred by time beyond recognition.
      The girl's cries broke its sleep,
   but she stood dazed, without volition,
to watch that startled beast with the blind face
      circle within the rafter's slope.

"My hair! My hair!" she called, I wondering why
   the creature didn't swerve through the gaping
      squares of the unbuilt walls.
   Then, as though dreamt by my deepest sleeping,
our father sprang past us both; I wept to see
      him break the bat's thin calls

on the edge of a board—our fluttering death come home.
   As to the girl, all explanation
      only increased her fear.
   So the room that had held our visitation
fell to me, next door to whom she'd dream
      of wings tangled in her hair.

ARIADNE WITH CHILD

Straw-colored flesh and fur
rose up like animate earth
in falling Crete; the air
blazed with that blond myth.

We have sailed down tideless halls
of water where the prow's edge
carves Ionic capitals
across a glassy page.

Sea-shapes focus and blur,
but the god this clay contrives
wears a stubble of hair,
stays past the midnight, leaves

his living autograph
on the plains these farmers till:
five thousand years of chaff
he tramples to the soil.

And the hero's ship has sailed
northward to mortal shores,
while the lustral basins hold
dust powdered from the tears

these farmers' forbears poured
when the Minoan beast,
superb of thigh, upreared
to slay the regal guest.

Hero and brute still strain,
shape on muscled shape.
The woven maze is mine;
on drying blood I slip.

The animal will snore
this evening, muzzle on paw,
and the naked hero blur
into furrows the color of straw.

Lie quiet in my embrace,
beast and hero. I feel,
earth-born and brief, your gaze
cut black sails through the will.

CONJURY

1

    Laughing, the ghost
Billy Billigan sent me to find
    the condoms that always lay cached
in the dresser and with a pin give each the wound
    by which I might yet gain my lost
brother. My sister had done so to mend
    such a lack, he supposed.

2

    The girl lay stiff in her conjure-fit
    on the kitchen linoleum,
her face and shoulders taut with the pain of it,
    as the garbled voices came,
    troubling our breathless quiet.

    The afternoon
outside was bright with leaves aglow,
    fathers at work, wives gone
to their sewing circles, children free to play
    on every broad lawn's green,

    the house a prison then, though we
    stayed indoors, locked
to the shame and fear of conjury.
    "If I was ever waked
from the trance," she said, "it'd kill me sure, I'd die."

    And where does she unravel
the cord that connects her to a birth?
    In a wood? By a sill
that opens into a bestial myth
    for the hero whose kiss is fatal?

The family of ghosts I talked to told
    of a trail of guilts in mine.
Papa Ghost swore and Baby Ghost howled,
    "Billy Billigan's
sleeping with Mama Ghost under the bed."

Who says—hero or guard?—
"Beauty alone is the thing I came to kill,"
   as he stands in the central wood,
    yet seeing that the beast is beautiful,
      breaks his sword?

    The leaves fluttered mournfully like tongues
      beyond the window panes.
Had prince with his lady passed, who'd have seen his wrongs
    lumbering behind in chains—
   that body worn once, bright as fangs?

    We are three, I know,
  and I wait in the dark, imagining
   suitable ends to the play:
Lady and beast one, another lady and princeling,
    or beast embracing his foe.

Heroes at any rate connect
    the waiting brute
and the sleeping girl I bent to wake,
   who would not die, she thought,
wondering only what penance to enact.

   She searched, then found a way,
and smiling, leaned up to be kissed—
    which to obey
denied the true nature of the beast
   I did not know till today.

    3

    Many a one
we led to his conjured violence,
   one house especially cursed,
two doors away, where Bill lived, an only son.
    He was in my confidence,
   just like a brother from the first.

   "We're conjuring in the garage,"
    I said that last time. "Stay
and you can sneak in later when the fit
   is on her and hear too." Urge

as I might, he rode his bike away,
    scared at the thought.

Whatever he meant, he sped
in perfect time to meet the racing car
    and lie dismembered. One wheel
still whirled crookedly when his dad
    from the porch door
had reached the spot to kneel,

wet with the pieces he kissed at, as if a toy
    had broken. Wax disguised
the damage at the funeral,
    but one day,
before the road's stain had been erased,
    new tenants stood in that hall.

I told their one child, Ron,
    the whole affair. He eavesdropped when
        Bill cried from the trance,
"The wax has melted, the pieces run,
    living, under the stone."
Neither of us enjoyed the April rains.

Though older, he joined the scouts—we hiked
    in every weather—
but wouldn't kneel with us at the fire
    where each at his own sex worked
to be first at winning his spermless spasm. "There's better
    things than hands to wear."

I saw his face
    long after conjury died out,
        printed with the story
of an exploding grenade he lay across
    to save his fellows. No doubt
some few tatters were found to bury.

Both houses have long ago been leased
    to strangers, breaking bad luck,
and his voice comes, not from a ghost we conjured there,
    but from a childhood past

    when darkness led me to the dark
        garage to hear

  my sister's groans of pain
that always signalled the ending of a spell,
    and after heard him say,
  "Do you think there'll be some kind of stain?
      Good. Don't tell
  your brother how he was tricked away."

4

Had he lived, the doleful animal
    who gnawed the flesh of the young,
  would he have been content to maul
    dream victims, purring
by the fire, while his lady's thrall
    is broken by the strong
hero who loiters, like a ghost, in the hall?

II

Hippocrates demanded of him what he was doing. He told him that he was busy in cutting up several beasts, to find out the cause of madness and melancholy.
—Robert Burton

AN ARRAIGNMENT

The twenty-one men, unharmed, walk free down streets
where I have never been, fictitious country.
I can imagine clotted patches of flowers
springing from the spot in Philadelphia
where how many men in a circle smile to see
their captive's flesh gape back in link-shaped patterns
at each fall of the chain, laughing to hear
(as how many pairs of eyes roll back in pleasure?)
bones shatter beneath the flesh. Only one was beaten.
      Three were killed. I was not there.

I cannot testify. It would be hearsay
to detain the killers with my curse.
No blood-nourished flowers profane that landscape
where twenty-one men set out to do a duty
and now go free to tend their wives and prisons,
two of my race not even given the right
of their earned beating, of suffering equally
before their death, but kept alive to hear
a friend cry out for them *their* pain, unsuffered,
      forced to bear witness. I was not there.

How little we have of their fictitious death,
not even sure of the spot, no wiser century
able to build its marble anger there.
What thicket or clearing arched by what spring branches?
What slant of sun or moon looking through a knot
of how many men? Twenty-one, let's say—whose shadows
slip closed on three dissimilar faces lit
with the dwindling hope that this will surely be
another mere annoyance. A chain glints upward.
      Links poise—and fall. I was not there.

We live in a northern slum. But the hungry child
next door has already grown unreal to us.
His fever-sores, his roach-infested sleep,
the flowers of blood knives sow upon the asphalt
are as fictitious here as Philadelphia,
stills from some 'thirties movie. We've seen it all.
"Only the squares go down to Mississippi"

—which is all right, a senator says, if they
obey the law, obey the chains that flash
    in Neshoba County. I was not there.

Of course they washed their hands in Philadelphia
before they sat down to belated suppers,
before they mounted their wives in bed that night
with unexpected ardor. No spoon or sheet
knew the frailest bloom of blood, none of it mine.
And why do I start just now to hear a child
cry out in sleep a block away, a flowerless
block of asphalt unstained with my blood?
I am not here. I am twenty-one men who walk
out of a clearing with unspotted hands.

THE CANDIDATE'S DREAM

Thousands of ballots held my name,
but what the office was nobody knew.
The electors in the congress of my skull
were to convene beneath their marble dome
and vote for extinction or survival.
They would not say how they were pledged.

I campaigned through the suburbs of my sleep,
telling them how worthy my voice was
of all their x's, but when they asked
how I would vote on enemies and issues,
words would not come. Their eyes were strange.
They kept their children from me.

Back from the tour, I stepped down from the train
to see my opponent stalking through the depot,
his blind eyes glaring, his linen robes
matted with dirt, mouth flecked with foam.
His gnarled hands writhed along the staff he leaned on.
He looked the other way and would not speak.

That was last night. Now, before this real assemblage
that I must dictate to with foreign threats
and vague prosperities, how shall I cry out
"I do not wish to have your vote,"
for fear my opponent, that other self,
be carried on the shoulders of this multitude?

IS AND IS NOT

The malingering Private Is
eyes his rifle bore,
toe in the trigger, while
the Northern Lights glare.

In another town, Miss Is Not
crawls raped and bleeding to church,
lights a candle and stabs herself.
Through Is and Is Not I march,

seeing the mouth of a bullet
opening lips upon an eye
that hears the dark burning
dazed icicles gray.

I nuzzle the soldier's breast,
freeze her wickt hand.
In waxen fragments
that wane blue-blind,

I taste their wound bones glowing
a ticking wheel
that for an instant
six hands roll.

Is it their shadows or light
curved upon itself
that explodes rose windows
in the gulf

between a soldier dying
and a dead girl, forced?
Love kills itself in spirals
from which stars burst.

THE COURTIER

From the back window she watched the man
through bars she had installed the week before
    as he leered squat-haunched on the tar
of the roof. She lifted up her ice-and-gin
    but saw it turn rust-red in air.

    Out of eyeshot
in the kitchen, she heard the dangling phone
    still clicking of its right
to give her the words of some lewd threat
    that waited on the line.

She searched the ice-box for something still
    unmolded for her cat
who screeched, locked in the bathroom, that its meal
was long overdue. She touched the rancid meat,
    then went to her post again and sat.

Soon she heard the creak of steel
    on steel, his painstaking work
resumed: she breathed at every rasping stroke
    with which he made the file
    sigh like a lover at the rail.

    In her mind an orange fire swam;
    she saw the navy-blue police
joined with every black-jacketed hoodlum
    through those acres of slum,
brandishing knives in every unscarred face.

Even now their blurred tongues on the wire
    could not diagnose her call.
In a hundred languages they swore
    she had nothing to fear.
"Buzz, buzz," whispered the file.

She foresaw herself opened with one blow,
    like the rind of a ripe fruit.
The purring cat behind the door would prate

of acrid delicacies to claw
    and partly eat.

Crawling to the window she showered in her dream
    all her keys
    and hidden eyes on him,
crying, "Manuelo, stranger, brother, climb
    my rusting balconies.

"See the thrown flower of my blood
I wore at my ear as a sign for you.
These bars imprison us both. And yet put through
    the scarred hand I may wound, but hold,
    though all the tear-shaped bombs explode."

The refrigerator answered with a whir,
    too late to save its spoiling sweets.
    But the cat and the phone roused her
    to hate gnawing at its last bar,
and a confusion of voices in the streets.

EMISSARY FROM A WAR

Walking on the darkest shadowed
path, you meet a crippled stranger.
The newspaper on the tea-tray. Did you

forget the face that stared at you
obedient, naked, bleeding, gasping
beside the curled peel of an orange

for one breath of the air you breathe,
fallen to the grass, the head
still wet, all black its printed blood?

Now he stumbles toward you over
more familiar ground, to stand
looking down at you as into

an open grave, his open sockets
pearled by the fountain's tears, not yours,
or did you forget that he would meet you

on this shadowed path, to ask you
for directions through the garden
(no flower but has been part of him),

obedient, naked, bleeding, gasping
for one breath of your air. You breathe
away his life with every heartbeat.

      Yet he is here.

A BIRTH

In the night the mutilated bodies of the dead swam by,
each bearing the mark of his fatality.
"Will you never have peace?" I asked that swelling river,
watching the money their slashed veins spilled
rise to the bank I lay on, powerless as ever
to purchase their freedom from hunger or desire.

I wondered then at one of my old notions:
that every malformation in the flesh
each man writes there himself—the mind's characters
illuminating the pages of his body.
"This I got from my fathers," called one of the dead,
"and this from the festering borough where I lived."

Then the current cast one of them up beside me,
limbs perfect, flesh unmarred by any defect.
We lay together on the bank a moment
above the accusing waves. I touched her side,
round with the lift of breath, felt her heart
singing through the meadows where my hands pastured.

"How did you die?" I asked, "or come to be
among the dead?"
     "The world has not yet stamped me
with its resistance; time, thirst, hunger,
fear, and longing have never pressed against me
in definition. I search among the dying
for features," and bent above me her faceless head.

My lips left marks like wet bruises on her flesh.
Eyes, nose, and mouth appeared. Her body
shuddered with birth. I kissed her into life.
But as she rose from the bank, no longer perfect,
the dead flowing past cried out, "They're cheating us!"
then pulled me down, groaned once, and at last lay still.

III

One short and obscure statement in Vitruvius . . . had a decisive influence on the Renaissance. . . . that man's body is a model of proportion because with arms or legs extended it fits into those "perfect" geometrical forms, the square and the circle. . . . Taken together with the musical scale of Pythagoras, it seemed to offer exactly that link between sensation and order, between an organic and a geometric basis of beauty, which was (and perhaps remains) the philosopher's stone of aesthetics.

—Sir Kenneth Clark

THREE VISITATIONS

Upon the threshold of my sleep,
borne from the limen's overflow,
Vitruvian man arose from where
he labored at the mill with slaves.

And I saw limping beggars lift
their bowls of sores like roses when
that glad day struck these avenues
with his *sol justitiae*.

Before my door he sang how suns
lay hid at the core of every stone,
how Eve, new-minted, rises up
singing in the tenements.

But I, enamored of the hand
that freed rough giants from their rock,
knew Buonarroti's prisoners
were the half he did not sing.

By evening that man blurred away,
dust-riddled on Scamozzi's page,
but a second angel sang,
struck-winged and beautiful, how love

must marry the perdurable.
And I, like Jacob, lay me down
in a foul bed to strain and gasp
against his lignifying gaze.

I dreamt again that inland lake
where water-lilies on the banks
are emblems of a world we lose,
but long for, far back in the mind.

And there they swim and dive, the children,
slender as birches, who will die
on foreign beachheads, chattering
across the littorals of sleep.

Then the second angel, too,
forsook me—like the bird that leaves
a wintry tree for that clear south
his songs in autumn postulate.

But you, the third and last, have come,
no dream or vision, but in flesh;
no cities gladden at your gaze,
no broken soldier blooms again.

Tommaso Cavalieri knew
the only mysteries you've guessed,
and he surrendered, after all,
a universal form to dust.

Yet be, as he, a link between
the actual man whose fleshlit grace
might borrow from the Phidian
and the dreamt, perfected pose,

and on the threshold where I breathe,
fountain to the wakened day
Vitruvian lilies, spread beneath
a sunlight that will never die.

TRAGIC ARCH

    Though I disclaim
the thing I saw, something in me
cannot disown its force:
an athlete seen lying on stone shelves through steam,

    propped by blind walls, a memory
    carved by the cloudy hues
along his skin, within which flesh turns marble,
    surrendered to the sigh

    of that enveloping kiss,
outspread so near abeyance, so immobile,
      that his gray features creep
in decade shudderings to face

what questions him if it could, his sex alone
    unchanged, like mounded grapes
    bunched ripening on the grassy thighs,
      not yet wine.

    Whenever I ask that shape
the sense of its averted gaze,
    I see the hand
held up to beckon me from sleep.

Like the marble Medicis
    or the bacchic wand,
he drives me backward into time
to solve his dream's disguise.

    For if steam thinned,
walls cracked, furled tendrils woke to climb
    across his graven day,
he be no longer stone, no more unmanned,

    brother to sister earth, his name
    would surge then through a sky
curved by clouded majesties and build
    the arch's leap for him,

>   on which the clear stone eye
>   and wand and tendrilled grape could loom, carved bold
>   above the human form
>   of lovers who must change and die
>
>   in an embrace the fatal earth has shared—
>   who hug, instead, the warm
>   cloth of his cloudy death to lie
>   walled, statued, cold.

EAGLE AND SPARROW

The eagle's tessitura lies beyond
the reach of any human will or voice,
thus not to be defiled by my hyperboles,
for which the common sparrow must suffice.

Yet the sparrow's very meagerness suggests
the thatchings of a truth the eagle leaves
behind him in his fierce swoop to the sun.
The sparrow stays domestic to our eaves.

So when we lie with dawnstruck lovers, he
is busy already, a part of what we know,
and like us, was not made to range the slopes
of Andean splendors, drifts of abstract snow.

Why then, waking alone, do I think of you
like an eagle whose beak has torn my sleep in two?

THE WER-MAN

She has smeared garlic against
every door in the house but the one
    that leads to her,
in the bed where each full moon has glanced
    at her scar-stiffened skin.

She knows I am her prisoner,
    that however long
I fight to stay in my basement cell
    starving rather than honor
her hungry need, my hunger shall prove too strong.

    Always the will
—or lack of it—fails me as before.
Yet I still remember the boy,
much older than I, who led me through the hall
    to his room, like this one here,

and folded and laid aside the few
    summer clothes we had.
His blond hair and body wore the moon
    so lightly that the blue
of every vein belied its red.

    By the blue of his eyes, how could one
have guessed what he intended, since here no beast
    had mingled its shape with his?
In an instant the thing was done,
    the jugular pierced,

the rich smell of my blood like the wet kiss
    that crept down to my thighs,
    as I bent weeping with pain to watch
        the joy-scorched face
mirrored in the moons of those blue eyes.

    After, for months I would not touch
        another's hand,
    bitterly fought what sent me out

upon my midnight search,
first to be wounded but at last to wound,

until the light
of the ripening moon would rub
my own face blond and blue,
and I wore an undying body to hook as bait
on my hunger's deadly barb.

She met me once like this and knew
a quick desire beyond
what even my disgust could guess at then.
She took me home to lay
her flesh bare to my tooth's demand.

And kissed at every stain,
and would not let me go, built my celled bed
so she could be assured
each month new mouths would gape and run
with richer red.

Her flesh, turned stiff now as a flowered brocade,
travesties my lust.
"Darling, I think of your own good,"
she says. "Alone,
your vice would mark each street you crossed,

their traps baited to cut you down.
Who else would *give* you blood but me?"
So she torments.
Yet deathless as I climb, the moon
blurs blue as a man's eye.

THE TOUR

The task seemed simple: to stand upon the platform
wearing the hempen robe they had provided
and stir at the narrow sluice of boiling lava
with a long wood pole. But as you stirred
the robe wore into tatters and you discovered
that its coarse fabric had absorbed all remnant
of flesh beneath until, like an emptied sack,
you slid in burlap fragments from the ledge.

Someone fell thus once or so a century;
others would pause in their work—leaning to watch
the robe glow incandescent when it struck
the burning liquid, melt, remain a moment
a bas-relief of lava carved on lava—
then stir the surface to smooth whorls again.
No other sound than that hissing contact ever
echoed through the caverns where they labored.

The attendant smiled as he pointed this out—in the usual
five-minute tour that applicants were granted
so they might know the worst awaiting them.
Amid the bunks and showers of the anteroom
where we lay nakedly sprawled at ease, our arms
around each other, laughing, the tour completed,
he faced us again, unsmiling now, and said,
"Anyone who has changed his mind may leave."

A few did disappear into other chambers
to choose anew, but the rest of us lined up
to follow him past the pile of folded robes
and take our places at the chasm's rim.
Only with our first stirrings did we see
what the real task was: to let our weariness creep
in century paces upon us while we struggled
against the promised release, the ultimate fall.

HOMECOMINGS

1

Insensibly spreadeagled here,
    the body of this man
proclaims the animal vigor that his stare
      cannot contain,
    so marred, so broken,
no numbered harmonies construct the wish
    all outward signs awaken
  in the square circles of his flesh.

What worse a shipwreck, that leaves free
    the unbreached hull though all
within is ruined now? I look away
      before the spell
    asks me to wager
spent hopes that he might yet learn to forswear
    his alcoholic swagger
  and face the cold seas of the year.

Pythagoras copied such harmonies
    as numbered the eye and tongue;
beyond the square-joined circle, Vitruvius
      cast human wrong
    (or that arising
from flaws of misproportion). They did not see
    such outward beauty housing
  the darkness where this man must lie.

Yet here he lies: not dead, except
    to any hope or chance
that wakes his naked wits where they have slept
      and makes flesh dance
    upon new pulses
beating shoreward over sinking ships.
    No, only grief engrosses
  the brief pity of my lips.

2

Across from me you sprawl, your child
curled loosely in his sleep along the swoop
   of gentle power in your arm.

Music somewhere. Your wife sits veiled
in a gold silhouette, her shoulder's slope
   against the windowpane a form

of exquisite bemusement, eyes
trained vacantly upon the traffic's blur.
   I think how bravely she dared watch

a loom of bitter music rise
in fiery calligraphs against her fear,
   a weaving she could not unstitch,

but waited till the unprinted sea
might write the legend of your pain,
   knowing each crest you faced, each wind,

lifted you up only to view
more tasks unmanning you, never a sign
   of some calm island or gentle sound.

Music somewhere. And here again you doze,
   returned from where such grief had beached
your body's ruin as I, though unrecorded,

doubted my kiss could rescue, giving your eyes
   this wakened sight, like gold rays stitched
through the cloth Penelope unbraided.

Music. I listen. Telemachus sleeps on.
   And half-asleep, you sink to share
his mindless peace where melody turns myth.

Only your wife, above you both, will strain
   to watch those threads weave in the air
the final cadence, fray into a breath.

And I, who suffer wakefulness with her,
   having watched the castaway
repair his sails, set forth with no last look,

see it is I who am the Odysseus here,
   sojourning among strange loves till he
find strength to make the final voyage back.

3

Having excursioned outward from
the chartable currents of the human
through eddies beyond the farthest reach
ten fingers make in squeezing unfirm
winds to fists that batter through them,
now I make my opposing search.

Inward the land lies, until no gull
follows, or the salt-stained herb
of the sea disproves the landscape,
or both each other. Town after hill
after river backward until the barb
I cast pulls taut its humming rope.

Interiors more desolate than seas,
clapboard villages unlit by neon,
farmers with twangs I never heard,
in languages at last I cannot speak,
all, all bewilder, drive me on,
seeking a self in some strange chord

my salty hands could never strike
here in the tides of corn and loam—
and yet whose indelible notes are mine.
Perhaps one evening I shall stalk
a stray dog's cries beside the brim
of a fresh lake, hear some tavern

echo the final gutturals
of drunken men, now Elpenor,
now Ajax, drink ablutions of rum

instead of blood to see behind walls
a dozen rivals round a whore,
knives bared, and know I have come home.

IV

He was now past the healthful Dreams, of the Sun, Moon and Stars in their clarity and proper Courses. 'Twas too late to dream of Flying, of Limpid Fountains, smooth Waters, white Vestments, and fruitful green Trees, which are the Visions of healthful Sleeps, and at a good distance from the Grave.
—Sir Thomas Browne

I have also realized that one must accept the thoughts that go on within oneself of their own accord as part of one's reality. . . . The presence of thoughts is more important than our subjective judgment of them. But neither must these judgments be suppressed, for they also are existent thoughts which are part of our wholeness.
—C. G. Jung

THE DECORATORS

    We did things second best, used glue
        and old electric cord
instead of nails and picture wire. We shellacked
        only what floor showed through
    after the rugs were down, and said
            we liked the effect
we got when nothing was left to do.

    For a month or so things were fine;
friends ooh'd and ah'd the right amount, we thought.
        But imperceptibly
    the house of its own accord began
        to show its doubt
concerning each device that we
        especially doted on.

Banister rails fell loose; shelves sagged; boards
        groaned in the night and broke;
    mirrors at first made no replies
        to faces proffered
in the strongest light, then cracked,
        weary of their lies;
the floors warped like a grin at what we'd dared.

    But not until the ghosts
themselves screamed up and down the stairs
        did we begin
to argue who'd most feared the cost
    of sound supplies. Both swore
the other was guilty of each current sin
        the sly house had devised.

    Devised to test us, probably—
        but I, the last
    to weaken, could take no more. I packed
        those things that seemed to me
untaintable and left to sue for rest
        in every room I picked,
        tossing in each one sleeplessly.

       I lay in wait
  for the loss to snake after me in good time,
     half a caduceus
wound writhing on the path of my retreat.
   I heard its slithering climb
    to where I hid from it. Its hiss
       filled the whole street.

Yet it cured nothing, only bore
  me back to haunt a house,
ruined and deserted, where I lurk
    within each shattered mirror
     for bargain-hunting visitors
       willing to work
things right again, as they were before.

FAREWELL IN A DRY SUMMER

Listen: something is very quietly ending under these trees.
Here in the gathering afterglow as I stand,
listening for the word that wanders deep within you
and cannot find the roadway to your tongue,
I have the time to muse
on the mere collision of particles in sunlight,
think how hand touched to hand is a dull friction only
giving its little warmth, answering nothing.

Listen: something very silently draws to a close now.
Counting the pickets in the fence, you do not say
each step I take along them is space enough
in which to deny my hands that tremble
to be green roots probing deep through the speechless earth.

Listen: something is very softly ending between us.
I know how the dry moths of your eyes,
fluttering to be free from so much seeing,
will fly off into the thickening dark some sunset.

Listen: something is very quiet between us now.

FUN HOUSE

Of all the phantoms from my first year in the city
—all of us young then—I've thought most lately
about Celia, a square squat Lesbian
who alone among that zany crew
disliked me utterly no matter how
I tempted her with tidbits of affection.

I suppose now she surely must have seen
invisible tremblings in the face of stone
I wore as I wavered between two worlds, my voice
a querulous midwest twang. But I alone
moved from act to act that I had chosen
as though I might avoid some final choice.

She hated that, bound so to her desire
by a bulldog body. I found in her beetled stare
the scorn of every woman who had said,
"But I don't *love* you."
                          Once, at the Palisades,
we went to the fun house after an hour of rides
to see what freaked selves we might find mirrored

in the rubbery glass. One of them made of us
laughing beanpoles whose Martian bodies rose
pitifully skyward. Then Celia took her place
—to see a lovely stranger, gaunt and tall,
stare back at her, womanly, more beautiful
than any who had lain in her embrace.

The silence frightened us. And then the eyes
of the mirror-woman filled with tears,
breaking the spell. Laughing, we turned away
quickly to other games the years would win.
For choice by choice the heart has had to learn
what Celia chanced in a single glimpse that day.

UNDER NEW MANAGEMENT

I went to the offices in my brain
and stamped my foot and raged and roared,
"I won't put up with this! You men
have bungled everything you tried."

They took their horn-rimmed glasses off,
tugged at their collars and looked hurt.
Their answer was to hem and puff
as though faced with an idiot.

"Get out!" I cried. "Pack up your junk—
you're fired." Then I stalked out, unsteady
though borne up by my rage, to slink
around the garden of my body

where lions slept with lambs in bowers,
hawks nested with wrens. When I came home,
back to these lightless corridors
untenanted of any claim,

I saw that the offices were bright
behind locked doors, filled with a noise
of snuffling muzzles and clawed feet
and contests of inhuman voice.

I smelled the reek of rank wet hide,
saw dark stains spread beneath each door.
"What are you doing in there?" I called,
to get a raucous howl in answer.

That was some time ago. But soon
I walked my rounds by night, in fear,
setting before each lighted den
my garden's mangled provender,

to sweep aside the bones each day
from last night's meal, picked sparkling clean,
while wrens and lambs stiffen and die
in traps I set on the ragged lawn.

SERAPHIC COMBAT

If you would only once
show me yourself, then I could kill
    you or be killed,
no more to fast while desert winds
    rust the visored skull.

Once I thought I held
clues to your nature; like Apelles, sought
    piecemeal perfection's yield.

    Those fused parts begot
only parodies, unreal
    as nightmare's monsterdom,
unable to give or take wound but in thought.

So I chose Dürer's goal,
sought parts sprung from a central sum.

    But they, too, flowered
beyond the flesh; though whole,
    ungraspable: a bloom
to mock the armored body lust has bared.

Yet you laugh most to see me thieve
    the stunted hoard
of spoils too freaked for you to save,

for when I reach to claim that fruit
    you let some steel-keen glance
of your unbidden beauty graze my love,
    a stroke with which you start
all my wounds awake at once.

MEETING

Having begun to falter, she
swayed as ripe as any orchard
before the threatened fall of fruit
through a thin sky, blurring over
—taut with frosty promises—
behind curve-heavy apple trees.

Just waking from his wavering, he
scarcely could believe the fields
had slept so patiently in him
like hands laid palm up, undemanding,
ridged and whorled with furrows scored
by slant-veined skies about to shatter.

How (through gulfs of difference)
strangely two, unknown, will move:
more tentative than spring or fall
when both are held yet in abeyance,
more fragile than first yellow shoots
or the bronze skin of perfected apples.

Having just moved invisible inches,
they stare through silences yet unspanned,
heavy with earth-smells where a soil
holds tendrils scarring themselves toward light;
heavy with a dense completion,
as though they lay beneath bare apple boughs.

V

In the finer examples of the image of Mithra Tauroctonus the features of the god bear an expression of dolor and compassion as he drives the knife, and so takes upon himself the guilt—if such it must be termed—of life, which lives upon death.

—Joseph Campbell

DOWNHILL

    In the hilled leaf-heavy tree
    hung the colorless apple, deadly
       with untasted venom.
Two of the twining branches were mother and father,
    breeze-stirred against each other.
       They were human

    but hardly awake yet, though I played
    about the tree trunk. Leaves hid
       from me how they leapt and trembled
until the moment when a fresh gust
    cut the apple loose. It flashed
       and tumbled

    down to be cradled in their arms.
    The woman ate. The leaves in swarms
       bled over me
and the fruit turned crimson as it drew her life
    into the focus of itself,
       then fell free.

    I followed downhill as it ran
    its brambled course. I was the son
       who had no rooted ways.
I travelled, slept, and travelled. I lay beside
    naked men, sleep-carved,
       whose granite thighs

    enclosed my seed, then leapt awake,
    but whose blank faces were never like
       the man's my lost tree wore.
I rose to lunge downhill again and find
    my birthright in a gashed and stained
       apple's stare.

    Near the hill's bottom, young no longer,
    I found it lying. Perhaps my hunger
       could be assuaged at last.

With my first touch the empty shell decayed;
    I saw a stranger slept inside.
        I knelt and kissed

    her widening eyes that bade me take
    a ring of blood upon me as she woke.
        We felt in our lifted arms
sap rise. In me a lost man's semen
    quickened like breeze-scarred leaves the woman
        put forth in swarms.

ROUGHING IT

A brownstone simply disappears that was there yesterday.
Seven and a half children are born every second.
The new apartment house that takes its place
is for the half-child. The other seven
will crowd more densely the remaining brownstones.

Here in the country the advance is less apparent.
Look at those massive roots grappling a boulder
in their decades-old embrace. The seductive tree will win.
As we climb higher, the view broadens. Already
smudges of industry stain the horizon.

Some come here in trailers to play cards
about their Coleman lanterns, the old songs forgotten.
Transistors give them music. Chemical toilets
and bottle-gas burners keep them cozy.
I hug your body in the dark as we undress.

The shrill wind off the lake is music enough,
pungent with the smell of red leaves charring
slowly into winter, bitter with chills to come,
sharp as the cold thoughts that inhabit our night.
We lie on an air mattress, face up, the stars overhead.

We could not see them from our brownstone windows,
nor from the darkest street. A cindery ghost
of soot shuts out the view there that blazes beyond
as sun after sun our galaxy whorls out,
cooling sparks in the dead brain of a god.

Entropy: houses crumbling to rubble, farms
to cities, trees to farms, resplendent leaves
to compost, rocks and suns to dust.
And the seven and a half children still crowd the ledgers.
A boulder groans open in the slow embrace of a root.

Suddenly I lean across to you, searching for your lips.
We understand the wind's language. Our desire

under these trees, beside this star-blind lake
can answer nothing but our own slow blurring
away into night and space and silence.

The cindery earth will drift like dust someday
around a burnt-out sun, its orbit unsteady.
Poor fools, our arching bodies locked in their fear of autumn
would kindle trees and stars to a permanent burning,
lit, unconsumed by the bodiless flame of their love.

SONG FOR LYING IN BED DURING A NIGHT RAIN

How can I wash the lightning away that shines on your closed eyes?
How can I tell the thunder to lie as calm as your hand?
How can I know two sounds as dry as your voice before love and after?
How can I fear what I have never seen in your face?

Street noises ascend from the city beneath us
as the rain falls—sounds that merge and blur through my gabled window
to reflect the danger all my asphalt nightmares proffer
without the slow pulse beside me of your sleep.

But who are these bleeding strangers, naked as shadow,
who stalk at our bedside, calling your name?
When I look their faces gleam brittle with lightning,
exposing an instant the white harvest of your flesh.

Why do they curse our handclasp? How have we hoarded
what fills their hunger, what falls like rain from their wounds?
Why do you lie unmoved like mounds of fruit and let their kisses
crawl red and wet across your ripening face?

How can the rain wash away such stains as your lips wear?
How can I tell their scars to grow smooth as your skin?
How can I know two sounds as dry as your voice before fear and after?
How can I love what I have never seen in your face?

RITES OF PASSAGE

For years I fashioned only jerrybuilt dream-
    hulls of manliness
  that no bellied sails became,
    till valleys of rivered thighs,
      hilled chest, burled arms
  were the sole landscapes that could raise
    my expeditioning eyes,
longing to love the shrouded father whom
    no prayer could claim.

    Others stayed home, found out
  so near at hand in youth the joy
    I scaled so late:
familiar as jokes to act in the cut hay,
    known as a summer night
  the years eroded, its bed run dry.
Why do I rise more man than they to know
    my hard delight
  knock now at the moist gate?

  Slowly because my flesh has learned
to chart within itself a burrowing male
    no search could find
  beyond, nor feminine yielding swell
    to climb but in a strained
mimicry of lust. I hail
    new shores to feel
an inward man and outward woman bound
    for their undreamt-of land.

    Now the frown
  of my ghost father fades. He roars
through veins he never guessed his smile could burn
    far from his mountainous snows—
  but leaves me as I wake to lean
naked in my defenseless lunge across
    her meadows—for not years
    of dreams may own
their mystery, no, nor the lips, rod, arms of man.

MOVING OUT

Our neighbor downstairs is moving
after wishing us ill for more than a year.
At first he played his Bellini operas just for fun
but later because it shook the whole house
when we were trying to read or write or make love.
He said he'd exchange his silence
for fifteen hundred dollars.

Tonight my wife, unaware, lies asleep upstairs
while I sit here—with a butcher's knife on our oak table
and a bucket of water in the vestibule—
waiting for him to climb the stairs
and set another fire against our door.
Why should I care? We didn't pay money we didn't have.
We ripped up our floorboards and blasted him with Bartok.

I used to be a Quaker pacifist, long ago in college.
I think of Jews with bowed heads walking naked to their death.
In the packing plant I worked at, lambs were hardest to handle.
They didn't fight back. They didn't believe in evil.
One blow of the hammer settled it.
Certainly I am a coward, but still, but still,
if I am to die that way, some will die with me.

Last night Malcolm X was murdered while our neighbor
set fire to crumpled newspapers at our door.
Malcolm would not have gone to the crematorium
like the lambs, though he stood unarmed at his last podium,
preaching a new doctrine that in time
might have led him to love or thereabouts.
I have this knife. I am brave as a Quaker lamb no longer.

This morning we went out down the stairs;
I tossed burnt newspapers through the stairwell,
kicked at the dogshit he'd scattered through the hall.
My wife helped, trembling. All her life so many people
had claimed to love her, thus excusing the atrocities
they cheerfully performed upon her: mother, father,
lovers. Her answer was to strive to love them back.

Now she struggles to share my hatred, too,
who has not seen lambs hoisted by their hind legs
to the moving rail, who wept for Malcolm's murderers.
God, may this knife tonight rust unused in my hand,
no fires be set against the love we struggle
to share in spite of all our time's murderous cowards.
Listen. I hear his footsteps climbing up our stairs.

THE BULL-KILLER

My perishing body that thought
only to kill or be killed
—the father destroying son—
now learns its hardness best
glitters like knives or horns
encircled by the arms
of a woman who marries my death.

Armed with torch and knife,
the god, born from her rock
by a tree where a fresh stream flows,
comes to affirm the cruel
dying of the world's creatures,
the smiling moon-bull gnawed
by the lion-bird of the sun.

In the shallows of Snaky Creek
I shivered naked from swimming
to watch dull-witted crawfish
nip at an offered stick.
I found a hollow snake-skin,
crumbling already, a silken
memory of a dead summer.

Weekdays, I pushed the warm calves
from the kill-room into the freezers,
their blood clotting my jacket,
shoulders wet to the skin—
initiate of life and death
as though I lay in the trench
bared to the bull's hot gore.

The wings of the seasons curve
from the snake-wound lion-man,
his own caduceus,
healing the death he deals
his crescent-horned host.
Rooster, pine cone, and dog
attend the terrible rite.

The athletic god must lug
the live bull from the light
so only a torch will tell
the knife's arrested flash
downward into his throat.
A scorpion bites his testicles.
His blood flows out as grain.

Who claimed such transformations
come only to elude
that god's embrace? Surely
he reveals himself
more than a coupling beast.
I see the sorrow on his face
as his blade sings through our flesh.

It is only two decades since
father and god and bull
made war on sanity.
I stand in the slaughterhouse:
I am its sewers and walls
at which the dying claw.
I bless the knife's fall.

The young bull-killer wore
a snake-supple body
maned blond as the sun,
flaked blood on his fingers
while he ate his lunch and gazed
over ripening cornfields, face
haggard yet from the kill.

Shape it with tongs and hammer,
the crippled life he devours,
time's endless coilings tempered
by sunfire and the tides.
Yet I tended that slaughter of innocents
while men by the millions were gassed
or melted to ticking statues.

Her arms are not enough.
Murder and death are not
identical. We stretch
our necks too eagerly
to our time's choice of evils,
fearful that pain and love
are untranslatable.

Up, down, sunrise and -set,
the casting off of a skin,
the sharpening of calf horns,
the bull's sperm bright as the moon.
Crows crowd to peck at his offal.
The curved lunge of my spine
bites the apple of my brain.

My body blazes, expires,
in her moon-embracing flesh.
We couple but to kill
and yet I was that god
and am this man she carries
down to the torch-bright grotto
where god and bull must die.

At the bottom of the trench
his hot blood spatters me.
Invisible filaments
pierce through my skin and burrow
deep, deep through the earth.
I am stitched back into her body.
I hear her pulse. I live.

VI

Come from the wombe of night, assist a maide
Ambitious to be made a monster like you;
I will not dread your shapes, I am dispos'd
To be at friendship with you, and want nought
But your blacke aide to seale it.
—*The Maid's Revenge*, Shirley

Nature, presently laying hold of what it so much loved [the bodiless mind of man], did wholly wrap her self about it, and they were mingled, for they loved one another.
—Hermes Trismegistus

NIGHTMARES

1

I am the man you know
as husband to your flesh, but in your dreams
    who are those doctors who
test your hunger for knives and flames?

    My dreams once seared
the moon's kiss on my brow and drew
fangs through my lips, my body furred and clawed
    until reclaimed by you.

Reclaimed? Then why does your sleep report that cold
    white room
where Venus and Isis, round with child,

    shudder to feel
lit blades, like fangs, strike home?
Your doctors wear my features as they kill.

2

Your doctors wear my features as they kill
    more than our love's embrace.
    More than ourselves cower at the wall
    to hear the fumes hiss.

Those nazis should be mine. They grin
from every villainy time can disclose
    since man thrust woman down
from the moon's throne and pyramids arose.

    Yet if I dream
beyond my own moon-punished face
    I see the same

    full breasts as yours and know
hips under me like yours. My thighs caress
    women resembling you.

3

    Women resembling you
are rare enough in fact. I choose

all kinds to play
my daydreams out. Dark, tall, with eyes

narrowed within a narrow head whose lips
smile slightly as we kiss.
She is the siren lady each man hopes
will be utterly his.

(I do not brandish a cat-o'-nine
to make her live.
Neither does she strain

to take your place in love nor to despoil
women I did not have,
men I slept with and love still.)

4

Men I slept with and love still
were not your kind
of decent nazi. Clown or fool
perhaps, longing to have a mirror for friend.

But that world, too, goes back
to myths before our blood: identity
of restless lack,
adventuring mind sharing one body.

—All false, I know,
for no shadow that I chose
on some blind street or dock but turned on me

my murdering werwolf's gaze,
waking your nightmare, at whose close
my old life dies.

5

My old life dies.
Weighed and found wanting, Isis calls.
Yet how much good dies, too?—the wintry seas
becalming the boat she sails.

Can Isis now reclaim the scattered man,
stitch, piece, and smooth

  his patchwork failures into one
  full-bellied breath,

 knowing she weaves in vain?
For docking at last in Osirianapolis,
  he puts her from the throne

and sends his moonstruck lust to lunge
  down streets of ice,
down avenues that do not change.

  6

Down avenues that do not change
my werwolves and your nazi doctors rove.
  Lying in bed we cringe
from every assignation they contrive.

  An absent father
called those lampshade faces up
  for your dreams to weather,
though they stop short of rape.

My moon-ripe sophistries, as well, limp home
  from rooms in which I stab
my father for his lack-love crime.

  But now they miss
old veins laid bare for them to rob.
My new self sleeps in riddles they cannot guess.

  7

My new self sleeps in riddles they cannot guess
  who doubt my watery climb
from death, made whole within a woman's eyes,
  unfanged, brought home.

 Yet gaining now the life I lacked
  sets up anew
 her doctors in unlocked
laboratories our acts of love supply.

  Look, I shall sentence them
to maim and anatomize each other
  beyond your dream.

And I shall guard and calm the strange
body of your love. I'll be your father . . .
    Who fathered this revenge?

            8

    Who fathered this revenge
would see us sway, drowned far beneath our love
        —unless we range
    farther than either ghost can thrive:

        back to the sea
        our motions fall and fill
nakedly of themselves all history
        over which we sail.

    Cut loose from personal past and care,
        the hull glides clean,
    takes us through estuaries, bays, coves where

love outlives us, where all dead lovers lie,
        eons back to when
our tribe from water slimed its crooked way.

            9

Our tribe from water slimed its crooked way,
        took the raw taste
    of air through burning gills, and grew
        beyond its thirst

    for salt spray's constancy.
Blunt-tailed at last, we learned to stand upright,
        a freak, gross and ungainly,
    hair replacing our scaly coat.

        No wonder beast,
    monster, werwolf walk our fear.
No wonder love remembers her who first

    from ocean rose to wield
all our best hopes. Naked, she walks ashore
        to build a world.

            10

        To build a world
    better than our fathers built

    would for that child
    have been short work. The fault
was with the animal she brought with her
    who would not be allayed
  with sleepy suns, with fruit, but tore
    wings from a bird
  simply for fun—until he found
in human pain a greater eloquence,
    then seized her throne and reigned
a world where many hunger to feed his lie
    of arrogance,
  where dreams and steel shut earth from sky.

    11

Where dreams and steel shut earth from sky,
    no place is ours.
  Derelicts, perverts show
torn faces scarred by soot, drought-shattered flowers.

  And armies march well-fed
past nations that starve—and call it peace.
    Why should our child
  be born conscripted to such a place?

Why else do nightmares, dreamt by times like these,
    rise undead from their grave
to mingle with our shadows as we kiss?

    Their eyes illumine
  night torn from day, desire from love,
    man from woman.

    12

    Man from woman
    had his birth. I steer
back to that watery rising for an omen
    by which to survive this war.

    I see her anadyomene
    at the shore's edge,
  wringing her hair. Our pulses know
this is the clue that answers all our rage.

I see her walking blank
deserts to recover me from ashes
    so she can link

  the dead parts back, the sails be spread,
    a boat that flashes
  but on love's full tide.

13

  But on love's full tide
will our undead lie dead at last? and we
    bolt the steel jaws gaped wide
  to snatch our unborn child away?

    Groaning, we course
down launchways to the waves below,
shocked body to body, face to dreamless face
    that for the first time see.

And now we stare back empty, naked, real,
    and now we rock
on flesh that does not wince to sail

    beyond its limen.
  And now as we awake,
our nightmares rust away and we are human.

14

  Our nightmares rust away. And we are human
    to hope somehow that time
  might let us miss, as well, the common
    grief or harm

  that must await our sailing forth.
This avid century's ports are stronger far
    than any siege our worth
can lay to them, their war beyond our war.

    Yet let those fathers
of lack-love hone whole worlds awry.
    Their shadow gathers

  around a brave sail's glow.
You are the sea and ship I ride, and I
    —I am the man you know.

15

I am the man you know.
Your doctors wear my features as they kill
    women resembling you,
  men I slept with and love still.

    My old life dies
down avenues that do not change.
My new self sleeps in riddles they cannot guess
  who fathered this revenge.

Our tribe from water slimed its crooked way
    to build a world
  where dreams and steel shut earth from sky,

    man from woman.
  But on love's full tide,
our nightmares rust away, and we are human.

www.ingramcontent.com/pod-product-compliance
Lightning Source LLC
Chambersburg PA
CBHW031714230426
43668CB00006B/212